A World in Danger

WETTER

By
Brenda McHale

PowerKiDS press
New York

Published in 2022 by The Rosen Publishing Group, Inc.
29 East 21st Street, New York, NY 10010

This edition is published by arrangement with Booklife Publishing

Edited by:
Madeline Tyler

Designed by:
Gareth Liddington

Cataloging-in-Publication Data

Names: McHale, Brenda.
Title: Wetter / Brenda McHale.
Description: New York : PowerKids Press, 2022. | Series: A world in danger | Includes glossary and index.
Identifiers: ISBN 9781725336056 (pbk.) | ISBN 9781725336070 (library bound) | ISBN 9781725336063 (6 pack) | ISBN 9781725336087 (ebook)
Subjects: LCSH: Sea level--Climatic factors--Juvenile literature. | Floods--Climatic factors --Juvenile literature. | Climatic changes--Juvenile literature.
Classification: LCC GC89.M343 2022 | DDC 551.458--dc23

Manufactured in the United States of America

CPSIA Compliance Information: Batch #CWPK22. For Further Information contact Rosen Publishing, New York, New York at 1-800-237-9932.

Find us on

PHOTO CREDITS

Cover & Throughout – Sloth Astronaut, valterZ, Lukas Rs, JMCM, Fotokina, Gayla Worrell, 2 – Echunder, 4&5 – Rudmer Zwerver, S B Stock, 6&7 – Anze Furlan, Adwo, AMFPhotography, 8&9 – Hung Chung Chih, Tarcisio Schnaider, 10&11 – Genova, STOCK'BURIN, 12&13 – michelmond, Ihor Serdyukov, 14&15 – Phuong D. Nguyen, Hien Phung Thu, 16&17 – AJP, Sajeev K A, 18&19 – paul rushton, blphoto1, 20&21 – Alexandros Michailidis, ITTIGallery, 22&23 – PRASANNAPIX, polya_olya, wavebreakmedia.

Images are courtesy of Shutterstock.com. With thanks to Getty Images, Thinkstock Photo and iStockphoto.

CONTENTS

Words that look like **this** can be found in the glossary on page 24.

ARE WEATHER AND CLIMATE DIFFERENT?

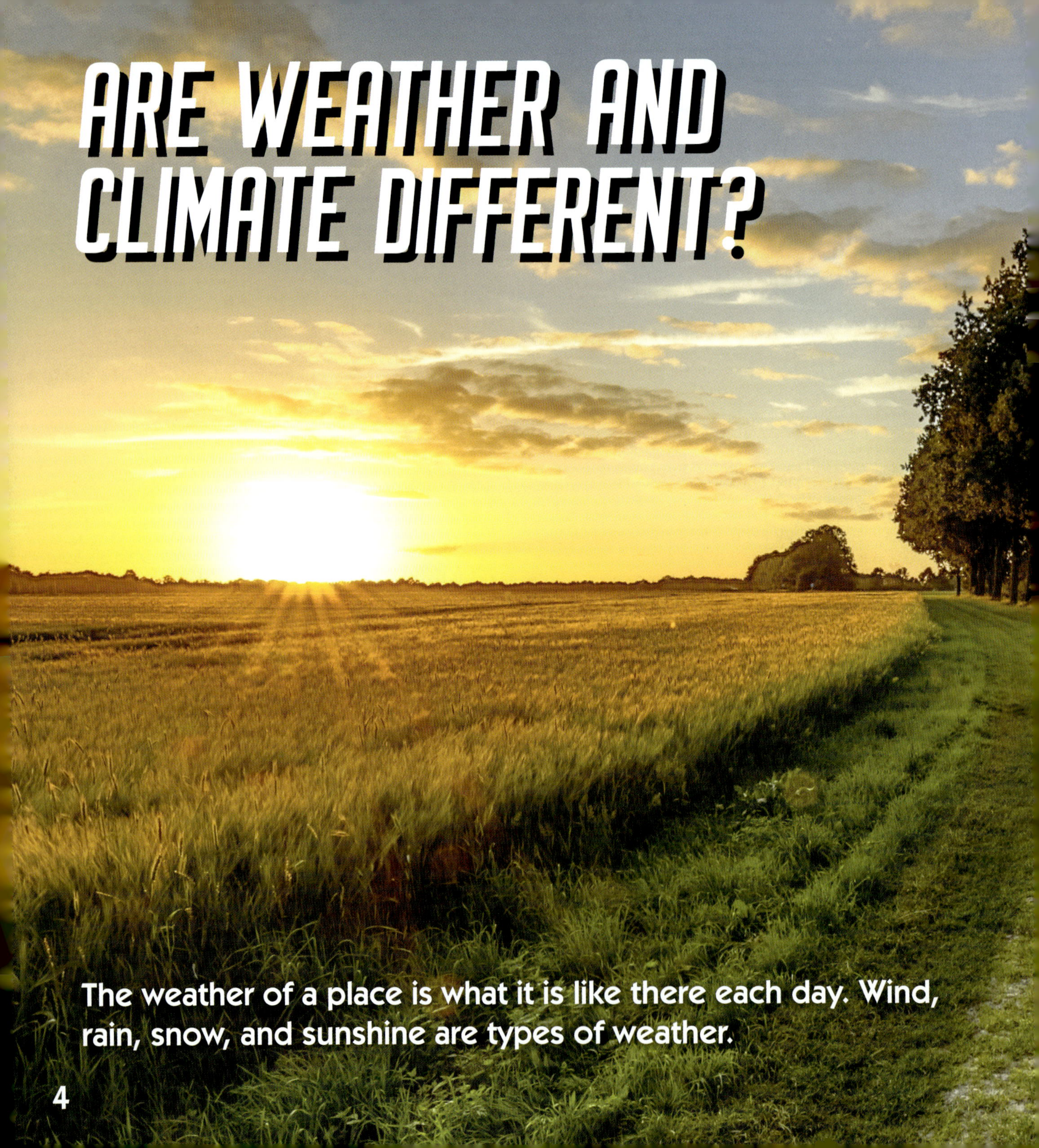

The weather of a place is what it is like there each day. Wind, rain, snow, and sunshine are types of weather.

Climate is what a place is like over many years. If a place is hot and dry, it has an arid climate. It might still have rainy weather now and then, but its climate is arid.

WHAT IS CLIMATE CHANGE?

The climate is changing all over the world. Global warming means that Earth is getting warmer. Scientists think it is getting drier in dry places and wetter in wet places.

Many places that used to get some rain are getting much more now. It isn't getting wetter everywhere, but rainfall is getting heavier in lots of places around the world.

WHY IS CLIMATE CHANGE HAPPENING?

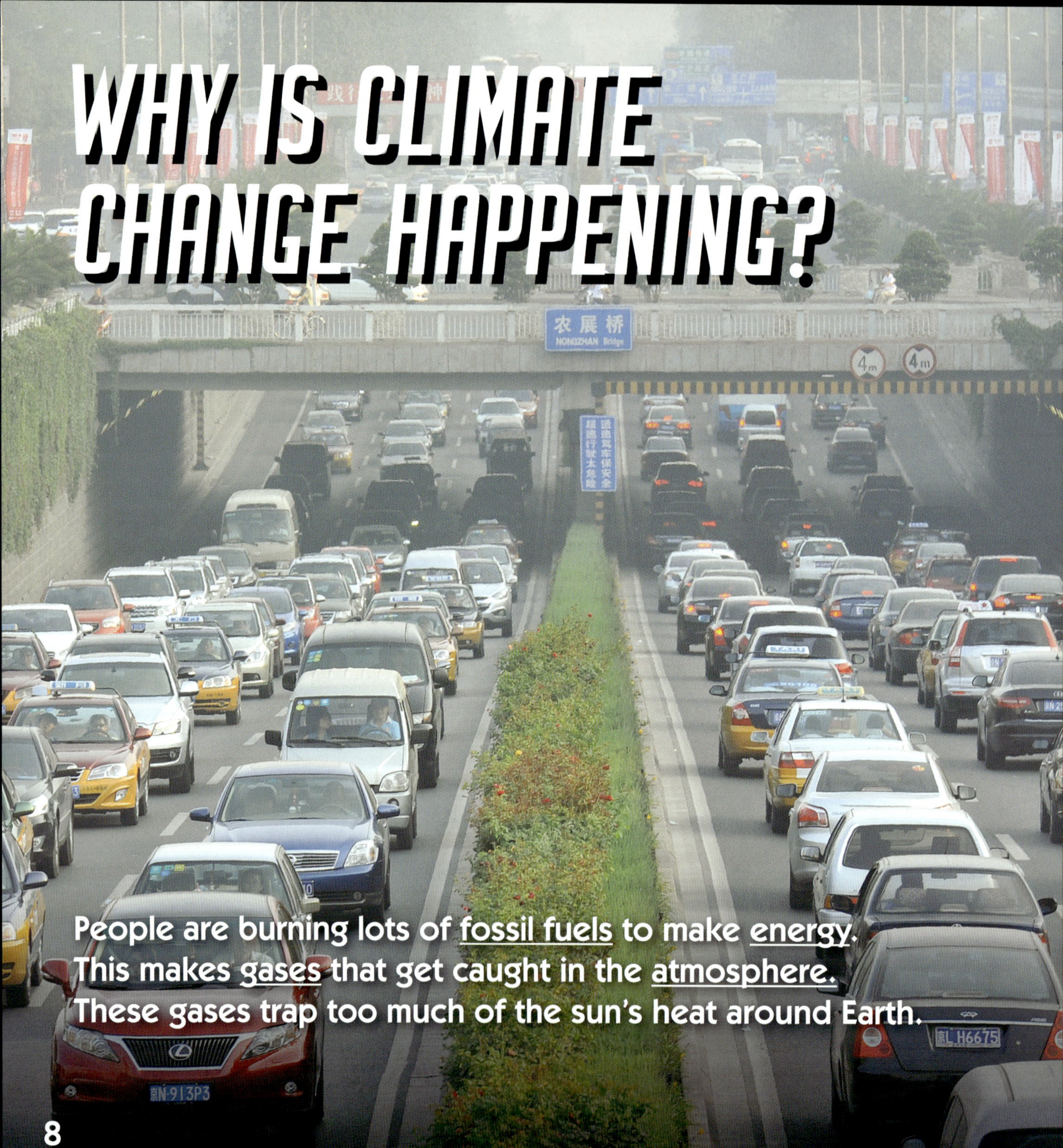

People are burning lots of fossil fuels to make energy. This makes gases that get caught in the atmosphere. These gases trap too much of the sun's heat around Earth.

People chop down or burn big areas of trees to clear land for farming. Trees absorb, or take in, some of the gases fossil fuels give off. They can't do that if they've been chopped or burned down.

WHY IS IT GETTING WETTER?

The air around the world is getting warmer. Warm air moves upward faster and carries more moisture. It evaporates from the ground and bodies of water. The moisture comes together and makes clouds.

When there is too much moisture in a cloud, it rains, and the water falls back to the ground. This is called the water cycle.

WHAT IS FLOODING?

The climate changes all the time, but usually it is natural and happens very slowly. Now, it is being caused by the way people are living and is happening much faster.

When it rains too much, or lots of snow melts, a river may overflow and cause a flood. Sometimes the sea floods along the coast. This is happening more as sea levels rise.

Floods in Venice, Italy, 2019

MEKONG DELTA, VIETNAM

The Mekong River delta in Vietnam is nearly at sea level, so the sea can easily flood it. It is an important farming area. Salty seawater harms the growing rice, so if it floods, the farmers have nothing to sell.

Every year, the sea is rising by around 0.1 inch (3 mm).

A lot of people live close to the water.

The sea is rising because of melting ice. Warmer water also takes up more space than colder water. The Mekong River delta floods more now and it could get worse in a few years.

KERALA, INDIA

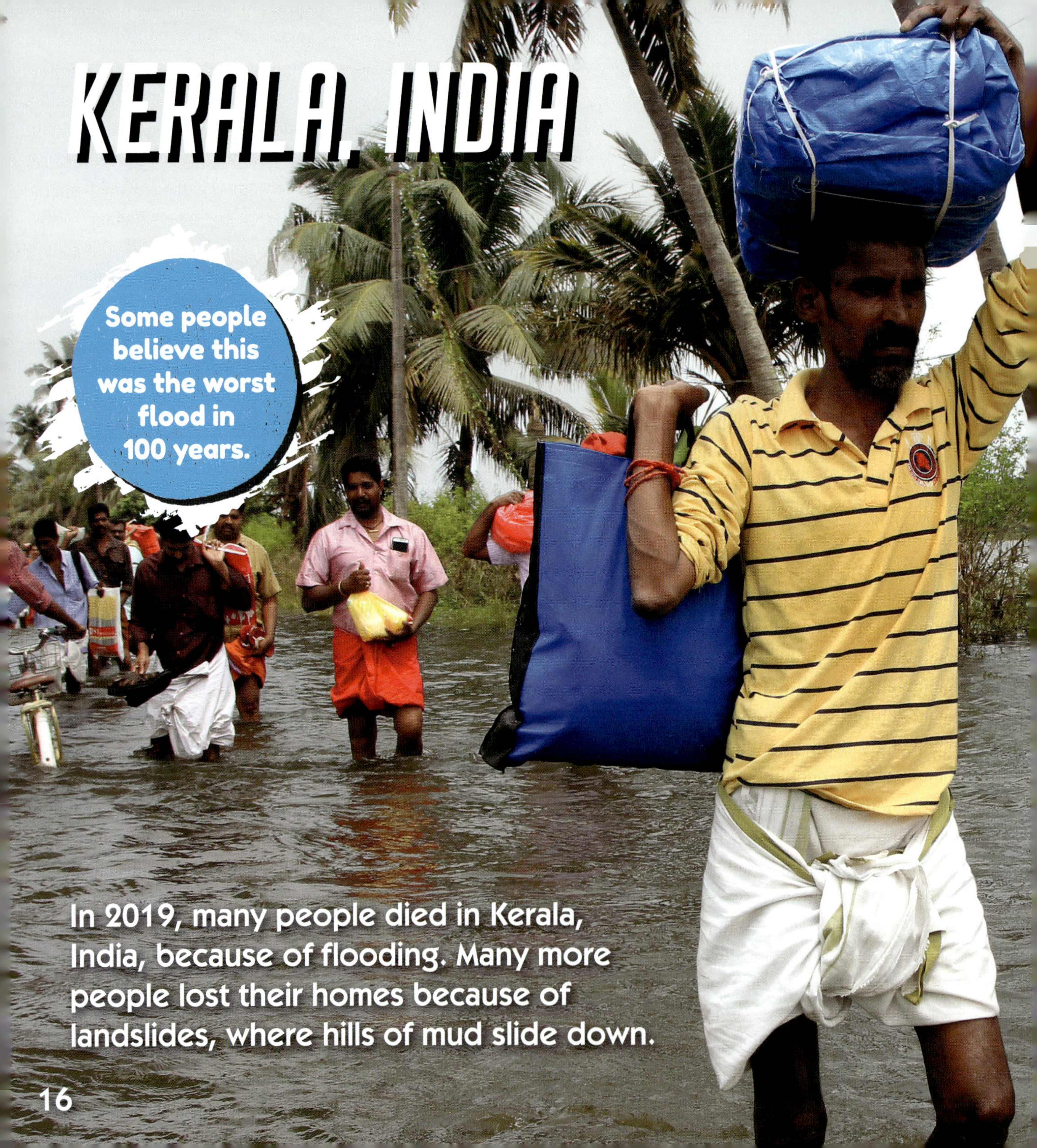

Some people believe this was the worst flood in 100 years.

In 2019, many people died in Kerala, India, because of flooding. Many more people lost their homes because of landslides, where hills of mud slide down.

Crops used for food get destroyed in floods, so people go hungry. Farm animals die or don't have food to eat, so there is no meat or milk.

FLOODING AND ANIMALS

When it floods, many small animals such as moles and mice do not have a chance to escape in time. Other animals' homes might get washed away.

Larger animals can also be affected by flooding.

Too much flooding can cause harm.

Flooding can sometimes be good because it adds water to the land and washes nutrients into the water. This helps fish and other creatures.

CAN WE STOP IT FROM GETTING WETTER?

To stop Earth from getting wetter, we need to slow down climate change. People are trying to get world leaders to make changes and laws that will help Earth while there is still time.

Many people are choosing to do things in new ways that can help the environment. If enough people do this, climate change can be slowed down.

Ask an adult about which things you can recycle in your area.

WHAT CAN WE DO TO HELP?

We can all do lots of things to cut down on the harmful gases that we are making.

Plant trees to help take in the gases.

Ask to walk or ride bikes places instead of taking the car.

Talk to your friends and family about how we can all work together to slow climate change. Ask your teachers to help you find out more.

GLOSSARY

atmosphere the mixture of gases that make up the air and surround Earth

delta a triangle of sand and soil found at the mouth of a river where it meets an ocean, a lake, or another river

energy a type of power, such as light or heat, that can be used to do something

environment the natural world

evaporates turns from a liquid into a gas or vapor, usually through heat

fossil fuels fuels, such as coal, oil, and gas, that formed millions of years ago from the remains of animals and plants

gases matter, like air, which fills any space available

hurricanes huge storms with very fast winds that move in a circle

moisture a small amount of liquid, such as water, that makes something wet or moist

nutrients natural things that plants and animals need in order to grow and stay healthy

sea levels how high the sea's surface is

INDEX